From Start-up to Success:

Navigating the Journey to Becoming

(And Staying)

A Successful Entrepreneur

.

FROM START-UP TO SUCCESS:

NAVIGATING THE JOURNEY TO BECOMING
(And Staying)
A SUCCESSFUL ENTREPRENEUR

By Melanie Colusci

www.fromstartuptosuccess.com

From Startup to Success Publishing
Pittsburgh, PA

For information, contact From Startup to Success Publishing at Melanie@fromstartuptosuccess.com.

Cover designed by Diana Stem www.dianastem.com
Printed in the United States of America

Library of Congress Cataloging-in-Publication Data

Colusci, Melanie
From Start-Up to Success / Melanie Colusci.
ISBN: 978-0-9992286-0-9
From Startup to Success Publishing

ACKNOWLEDGEMENTS:

To all the women who have supported me, held me up, been the shoulder to cry on, been my sounding board, and helped get me to where I am today—

Thank you!

While I can't list all the women who have been amazingly supportive, I would like to extend a special thank you to Jane Lerner, Shelly Lehrkind, Molly Sharp, Joan Ellenbogen, Li Connolly, Alexandra Classic, Kristin Tabbert, Robin Allen, and most importantly, my mom, Marla DeShaw.

TABLE OF CONTENTS

INTRODUCTION:

W hy did I decide this was important to write? Who am I to be the best person to write this?

As women, the hurdles we often face in the professional and executive world can be daunting. I have lived through inequality in the pay I received, double standards for performance, and in my industry, the proverbial "good old boys club." While it can be challenging to persevere if you are faced with these issues, it can be even harder if you are a business owner without a clear path.

Throughout my journey, I always wished I had someone to lead me and help make it a little easier. For that very reason, this was important to write. I wanted to write for all the other women out there who, like me, have faced challenges in their professional life—for the women building their businesses and craving other women to be their sounding board or their network of support or to not feel alone.

I don't consider myself anyone particularly special or an "expert" as a business owner. I don't have a degree in business ownership (not that there is such a thing). But I *have* lived it; I have somehow managed to (sometimes out of sheer dumb luck) survive and have built something special.

I want to share my journey with you to help you feel excited and supported on your path to success. While I can't protect everyone from their own set of challenges or making their own mistakes, I am writing this to help make sure you won't be unprepared or alone.

Being a woman business owner can be lonely without a good network of support. Throughout my journey, other women have been helpful and supportive and have been instrumental in my survival and success in my male-dominated industry. Without these inspirational and motivating women, I am not sure where I would be today.

However, what I didn't have was a guide *every* step of the way to help make sure I was doing the "right" things. There were times I felt like I had no idea what I was doing! I often found myself either naïvely trusting or stumbling into a situation. Both fortunately and unfortunately, I have had partnerships fail and have made a lot of mistakes. As I think back on my professional career, I wonder what a difference having this guide would have made.

So let's start with my beginning. Why did I become a business owner? Why have I survived and been successful?

I grew up in a small primarily ranching community in Montana, and people there know how to work. They work from the time they wake up in the morning until they go to bed at night. Montana is amazingly beautiful, but it can also be a harsh place. Maybe the work ethic I learned was a result of the environment or maybe it was from the survival instincts you need when you grow up in a family that owns a small business.

My parents weren't ranchers, but they did own their own business. For many years, my parents built and ran the cable television system for two small rural towns in the-middle-of-nowhere Montana. People definitely relied on my family to make sure they had their TV! As a result, so much always needed to be done. As far back as I can remember, I was "helping" my mom or dad either in the office or in the field. I vividly recall thinking I would NEVER be a business owner because of how hard they had to work. It seemed so stressful for them to not have a consistent paycheck coming in, knowing they had two children to raise and support.

What I didn't realize at the time was that owning their business also came with a lot of benefits. We were able to spend the summer months traveling or camping. We also got to visit many new places because of the different continuing education events they attended. Even though they had to work long, hard hours, they had the flexibility to take a few hours off during the day to participate in school events or help with an after-school activity.

They were able to create their vision of family because they owned their own business.

As I said earlier, I didn't set out *wanting* to be a business owner. It just kind of happened that way.

I started out on my journey working my way up "through the ranks." My starting place on this path was an hourly 8–5 position as an administrative assistant. Sure, there were times I had to work overtime and had what seemed like a never-ending list of things to do, but I really had NO idea, no clue what it would actually be like to have my own business.

As I think back on this, I was naïve and never appreciated or realized how comfortable being an hourly employee with a salary really was. I hadn't yet experienced the feeling of waking up every morning wondering what I was going to do to earn money for my family that day. I had no idea how hard being a business owner was. It wasn't until I transitioned out of my administrative position to a sales position that was 100% commission that I had a small taste of it.

Being in that sales position did help me start to understand and learn some of the important components of becoming a successful business owner. But, I wasn't there yet. After many years of trial and error and, more likely, sheer stubbornness and persistence, I woke up one morning and realized I had truly become that business owner.

It takes great courage for a woman to start out as a business owner or launch a business over a relatively short period of time, and because that wasn't my path, I have never felt what I did was anything extraordinary. Maybe it was purely survival. But, this is also exactly why I believe I am the "best" person to write this. I'm not anyone special or an expert business owner . . . but I'm tough and persistent, and I won't give up on you. I've made mistakes along the way, but by sharing my story and the lessons I've learned, I'm confident you will *feel the love and support you deserve*. It wasn't until today, this very moment when I shared my story with you that I felt I had accomplished something truly great.

I know this guide does not cover everything, as there are parts of this journey that I am still to discover, but it does help give you a good head start. This guide will give you some of the key components to becoming and staying a successful business owner.

So let's get started!

CHAPTER ONE:

HAVING A PLAN

Why is having a plan important? Some people prefer to live life by the "seat of their pants," while others prefer to plan every detail. Any type of person can be a successful business owner or executive, but to do so does require some kind of plan. In this chapter, we will discuss the basic principles of business plans and the importance of your mission and vision statements and goals.

I wish I had understood the importance of having a plan and the mission and vision statements earlier in my professional life. Had I understood it and implemented it earlier, I believe I could have been more successful. But, hindsight is 20/20. The past is the past. What matters is what we do now.

A plan is essentially the map or directions to the place you ultimately want you and/or your business to go. This is why a plan is so important.

I consider myself a planner. I like to have whatever I'm doing "mapped out" before I do it. But, for whatever reason, writing a business plan has always been a challenge for me. I guess you could call me more of an implementation person rather than an idea person. Give me the instructions, and I will make sure it gets done!

I have had to lock myself in a room, put my phone on *do not disturb*, and set the timer to make sure I get this piece done. Whatever it takes, DO IT!

Don't confuse "planning" and "implementation." They are two VERY different things, and we will talk more about implementation a little later. The business plan, however, is the set of instructions for your business or executive role, so no matter how hard it can seem to write, you HAVE to do it.

When writing your plan, a big consideration is the period of time your plan will cover. Many people work on an annualized basis or a 12-month period. But, I prefer to work with shorter time frames, so I write my plans around a 90-day period. I prefer the shorter period because it gives me the ability to reset and adjust more frequently. I also believe it creates more consistency in your results.

The majority of the world works on an annualized basis—which is fine. But think about it. If you have a deadline that's 12 months down the road, are you going to take care of everything for that deadline today . . . or midnight the day before the deadline? Imagine if you were running a race. Would you run *really* fast the entire time? Or would you run quickly for a bit, then jog, and not run really fast again until the very end of the race? If you are like me, you would run really fast, then stop, take a nap, look at the birds, eat a sandwich, and then say to yourself, "Oh shoot, I'm REALLY far behind. I better sprint to get to the finish line!"

Conversely, when working in a 90-day period, you sprint for 90 days, and then take a break. Sprint for another 90-day period, then take a break, and on and on until the end of the calendar year. It sure is easier to maintain my "speed" by taking four breaks throughout the year rather than procrastinating and having to sprint!

Because I can be a procrastinator, I work better with short deadlines. By giving myself the shorter periods of time to focus on my plan, I accomplish my goals more easily and quickly.

Once you've determined the period of time your plan will cover, you must create your mission statement. Your mission statement helps you communicate the long-term goals for you or your company. Some of the questions I used that helped me write my mission statement were:

- What does your company or you do for your customers?
- What do you or your company do for your employees?
- What do you want from your business?

The mission statement serves as a reminder to you, employees, and customers of the main purpose of your business.

Let's take a break. I told you writing a business plan is incredibly challenging for me!

Taking periodic breaks is a good idea. Get up, get out of the chair, get some fresh air . . . it helps keep your focus longer and your mind clear. I also like to set time limits for how long I work on a certain project. As an example, set a timer for 30 minutes and devote that amount of time to whatever you are working on. Doing that helps create an ending point so you don't feel like you can't do anything else.

Alright, let's get back to it. The next part of your business plan to consider and commit to paper is the vision statement. What do you envision your business or role in the company to look like in the future? This is what your vision statement should speak to.

Having a vision statement will help give your business or role clarity and prevent you from losing sight of what's important.

Your vision is the "light at the end of the tunnel." A vision statement doesn't have to be written for what your business looks like 10+ years from now. You can have multiple vision statements.

- What does your business look like in a year? Three years? Five years?

The most important part of your vision statement is that you connect with it. The vision has to *motivate* you; it has to *speak* to you. If you don't really connect with your vision, it will be easy to lose motivation and sight of it later.

- What drives you?
- What gets you out of bed every day?
- What are you passionate about?

When I left the sales position that started me on this path, in my mind, I held a vision of how my new practice would look. I could clearly picture it. I can see the furniture, the people, and the plants on the desks, the smell of the office and the signage on the door. When I think about this vision, I feel like I am actually in that place at that moment. ***This drives me. I feel this vision of my future practice down to the tips*** *of my toes.* Every activity I complete takes me one step closer to achieving this vision.

Here is an example of the mission and vision statements I wrote as part of my planning process for this book:

> **Mission:** To help educate and motivate other women so they can have successful businesses or executive roles.
>
> **Vision:** To create a network of resources for other women who want to be as successful as they can with their own business or executive role.

I have always been passionate about helping other women. As you can see, my mission and vision statements are simple, but I connect with them. I read these to myself regularly as it helps keep my focus and motivation.

When I had my first taste of being a business owner—in my past sales position that I mentioned earlier—we had a vision that we could never seem to achieve. We had the mission and the vision statements, but as I reflect on this now, we were missing clear, precise goals and tactics. We would talk about what we wanted to accomplish but did not actually write down deadlines for our goals or those steps that needed to be taken daily to get there.

You have to create and write a plan to achieve your mission and vision. These are the goals and the tactics that you need to complete daily to ensure your success.

Goals need to be precise, measurable, and realistic.

Remember this because it will be very hard to review your results later if your goals are not precise and measurable. I am absolutely a proponent of pushing yourself, so don't set goals that will be so easy to achieve that you've done it within the first week. However, it also does you no good if your goal is so tough that you give up.

To be clear: a goal is what you want to accomplish by a certain date, and a tactic is the activity you need to complete daily to achieve the goal.

I have a driver personality and have always been hard on myself. I've also been told I am hard to please. This might be because I set high goals for myself and have high expectations for me. How do I know what I'm capable of if I take it too easy? However, sometimes I set goals that were too high and knew from the beginning that it wasn't possible to achieve them. Instead of a challenging but realistic goal, it was completely outlandish. So halfway through the period I gave up. Why try if it's not even possible to begin with? Have you ever been on a diet where you were so super strict that you had no cheat meals at all for weeks? What happened? With me, I end up so tired of the diet and the restrictions for so long without any "fun" that I go on a full force attack binge-eating spree! This is the same thing. Your goals have to be challenging but realistic. It's all about balance.

Here is an example of one of the goals and some tactics I set for writing this book.

> **GOAL:** Write a book for women executives and women business owners that provides a guide to

establishing and maintaining a successful practice and career. Deadline: 12 months
TACTICS:
1. Create outline for book. Deadline: week one
2. Write bio. Deadline: week two
3. Write introduction section. Deadline: week three

Make sure that when you are creating your list of goals you don't write too many. Start with 3–5 goals to focus on initially, and add from there. Having too many goals can create diffusion and detract from what's really important.

I also want to make sure you know the difference between a tactic and a to-do item. A tactic is strategic; you planned this daily activity when you wrote your plan for the period. A tactic helps you achieve your goal. A to-do is what pops up throughout the day. To-dos are those tasks that need to get done at some point. They may have deadlines or they might not. I have an ongoing working to-do list that I keep on my desk and will cross items off as I complete them or add new ones as they come up throughout the day.

As women, our to-do lists seem to be never ending. It's hard for me to leave at the end of the day knowing I have 30–40 items still on my list. I also have to remind myself that it's unrealistic to think it will EVER all be done. I have found that I can more effectively get through my daily tactics and to-do list if I block out time in my calendar to work specifically on those items.

What is "time blocking"? It's basically the practice of blocking out time on your calendar each day to focus on one specific activity or action. Remember how someone recommended that I set a timer? This is the same concept. Time blocking is like setting the timer in your calendar throughout your day. It gives you clear start and stop times for each activity. Time blocking also helps with implementation. When it's scheduled in your calendar and treated like an appointment, isn't it more likely to get done?

Here is an example of one of my typical daily time blocks:

- ❖ 8:00 am – 8:30am Review goals and tactics
- ❖ 8:30 am – 9:00am Review and respond to client e-mails
- ❖ 9:00 am – 12:00pm Client meetings/phone calls
- ❖ 12:00 pm – 12:30 pm Lunch
- ❖ 12:30 pm – 1:00 pm Open
- ❖ 1:00 pm – 3:30 pm Client meetings/phone calls
- ❖ 3:30 pm – 4:30 pm To-do list
- ❖ 4:30 pm – 5:00 pm Open

When you block out time in your calendar, leaving some open times is important. Things pop up throughout the day that need to be completed the same day. You have to allow yourself some room for disruptions, urgent items, and taking breaks.

I am not great at saying "no" to people. I try to accommodate or help out however I can, whenever I'm asked. I will often stop what I'm doing—even if I'm in the middle of one of my scheduled time blocks—to take care of whatever the person needs help with. What I have learned over time, though, and what I am still practicing is saying the following, "I need about 10 more minutes to finish this. Can we chat then so I can fully participate and help you?" I won't lie: it's been hard to say this, but it's typically not a problem for the other person to wait a couple minutes. By doing this, it gives me the opportunity to finish my time block and be fully present with what the other person needs. Remember, if you do not control the day, the day controls you!

I find that when I am effectively following my time blocks, completing my tactics, and working my plan, my results are superior.

Some days, though, I seem to get too many disruptions or urgent requests, or I just can't get it together. We *all* have days like this. When this happens, do your best to stick to your time block and your plan. Remember, tomorrow is a new day, and sometimes you just have to GET OUT OF BED!

Being a business owner or executive is a lifestyle. You can spend all day every day working in your business if you allow it. But, *having a plan and working your plan gives you more flexibility, freedom, and rewards than you could ever imagine*.

Key chapter takeaways:

- Write a business plan
- Create your mission and vision statement
- Review your plan regularly
- Have clear, concise, measureable goals
- Time block!

Resources:

- *12 Week Year* by Brian Moran and Michael Lennington

- *The Secret* by Rhonda Byrne
- U.S. Small Business Administration www.sba.gov

CHAPTER TWO

REVIEWING YOUR PLAN/TRACKING PROGRESS

How do you know how far you've come if you don't know where you've been? What if you could make a slight change with one daily business activity and know what impact it would have in the future for your bottom line? In this chapter, we will discuss the importance of tracking your progress/results and taking time to review your plan.

I struggle with never really *feeling* like I accomplish much. But, often, how we feel and *reality* are two very different things. As I mentioned before, I have a driver personality, am a first born, and am from a small rural community (you worked!). In my mind, I never accomplish enough, and something more always needs to be done.

The year I moved to Pittsburgh from Montana, I earned about $6,000 for the ENTIRE year. This past year I earned, well . . . A LOT. It's easy to see that I have made progress when there is such an extreme difference between the two numbers. It's not as easy to see on a day-to-day basis or over a short period of time. For me, this is one of the reasons it's important to track my activities, my results, and what I've done.

Reviewing your business plan and tracking your activity regularly is important. One of the biggest mistakes a person can make when writing a business plan is to put it away and not read it again until the end of the year.

Have you noticed that most company's results are significantly better *right* before the end of the fiscal or calendar year as compared to prior quarters? Why do you think that is? I believe that most of us have some procrastination tendencies and decide it's time to "get to work" when the deadline is looming. It's this time of year when people pull their business plans out and try to accomplish all their goals. Remember college or high school and the long nights before the big test or paper was due? Remember all the cramming, re-reading chapters to help remember content, or writing the final 29 pages of the 30-page paper? It's the same concept . . .

I have a husband, three children, three cats, employees, CPAs, staff, and clients that I help or work with on a daily basis. I completely understand how easy it is to get caught up in the day-to-day and lose track of your goals. I mentioned before that I literally have to block out time in my calendar every morning to review my tactics and goals because it helps me remember what they are and enables me to intentionally focus on and work toward those goals. Constant progress is important, and it's hard to do that if you are always putting out fires.

My choice to utilize a 90-day period for all my plans/goals helps me feel more urgency to accomplish those goals. By working in a 90-day period instead of a 12-month period, I don't have the luxury of lots of time to get to something. Don't get me wrong. I still procrastinate with the best of them, but by shortening the period, I have found that my consistency and, ultimately, my results have drastically improved.

Just like someone who practices annualized planning, I will actually take the last week of each period off. During this time I do not intentionally schedule client meetings; rather, I use it to review my plan, complete any outstanding tactics, and write my plan for the next 90 days. I also use this time to make sure to-do items that I've been putting off don't roll over to the next period.

Remember, we will always have a long list of to-do items, so use this time to handle the most important or those you have put off for a long time. Use this week as your opportunity to "clean the slate" and start the new period with nothing hanging over your head. I like this break from the day-to-day as it gives me the opportunity to really work ON my business instead of always IN my business.

Some of the questions I ask while reviewing my 90-day plan and my business itself are:

1. What went well?
2. What didn't go well?
3. How do the results of my business tracking look?
4. If something didn't go well, what needs to be different over the next 90 days?
5. Did I perform to my expectations? If no, why?
6. What hurdles did I encounter that created challenges for me in completing the goals?

7. Can I put systems or processes in place that will remove those hurdles? If so, what does that look like?
8. What systems or processes need to be changed?
9. What systems or processes need to be added?
10. Did I take enough time off to recharge? If no, what will I do differently the next period?
11. What are the new goals I want to accomplish?

During this period of working on my business I also review and do the following:
- Finances of the business
    - Of course I review the finances for the business weekly, but during this period I look at the a bigger picture
    - Do I need to make changes to the budget?
    - Do I need to rebalance any of the debt positions I may have?
    - How does cash flow really look?
- Upcoming events/conferences
    - I make sure they are blocked out in my calendar and that I have completed all necessary travel arrangements and registrations
- Tactics/goals that need to be blocked out
    - I have a couple specific activities that I need to do quarterly for all my clients. I review the upcoming quarter and block out an entire day to accomplish this.
- Block out your time off
    - Even if it's just an afternoon off, it's still important to treat that as if it's a scheduled appointment

- Catch up on reading my work-related educational pieces
    - I get inundated with periodicals, e-mails, and other informational pieces that I *want* to read but never have the time to. I use this week (a couple hours of it anyway) to catch up on this
- Systems/Processes Review
    - Did any clients leave you?
    - If so, what was the reason? Was it a result of a breakdown in systems or processes? Should anything change?
- Review of your business tracking and ratios
    - Should there be a change in your activity for the upcoming period given what your activity was telling you?

Reviewing your plan is absolutely an important piece of the puzzle for any successful business owner or executive. But, like I said at the beginning of this chapter, how do you know how far you've come if you don't know where you've been? Let's spend some time now talking about business/productivity tracking and how this is *critically* important.

I was once told that I needed to run my business like a business. Out of context that seems like a very random statement but *it is THE statement you HAVE to live by*.

To run your business like a business, you have to track what's happening. *By tracking the activity of your business, you will be able to understand more quickly the expected outcome from any minor adjustments you make.*

Even if you are just starting out, tracking your activity and results is important. Here are a number of important items to track:

1. Your pipeline
   a. Being able to see what you are working on can give you an idea of possible revenue at any given stage in your process
2. Pace – the time it takes your process from start to finish
   a. This will give you an idea of when to expect revenue from that sale
3. Potential new clients – how many people are in your pipeline
   a. This is going to be important once you have some historical data as it will help with budgeting
4. Touches to prospects
   a. Tracking this will ultimately give you data that you can use to determine important ratios like how many prospects it takes to create one client
5. Meetings
   a. Tracking the types of meetings you have will allow you to see patterns. If you spend a lot of time in service type meetings, you shouldn't expect to see a lot of revenue in the next few weeks
   b. If you use a calendar, you can color code your meetings so it's easy to see the different types of meetings

          i. You don't want all the same color in any given week
6. New clients in a year and their demographic
    a. You will ultimately end up with a "target market" based on the demographic you most often end up working with. This is beneficial because it will show you the demographic you work with the best
7. Average sale
    a. By demographic
    b. Client ranking
8. Monthly or weekly revenue
    a. Useful for budgeting purposes
9. Ranking of client
    a. Will help in developing service standards
10. Actual results versus your goals
11. A number of different ratios
    a. Ratio of prospect to closing a sale
    b. Ratio of prospect to information gathering
    c. Ratio of information gathering to closing a sale
12. How many clients decided not to work with you or left
13. Total number of clients

If you are a brand new business owner and the above list feels overwhelming, pick three or four items to track initially, and then add to it. If you are starting out, at a minimum, track your pipeline, touches to prospects/clients, and types of meetings you have.

You really need to tailor your activity tracking to what's important to you or your industry. It will be different for everyone, but equally important regardless! If you don't know the statistics about your actual business, it basically makes your plan worthless.

The different business metrics that you decide are important can be tracked in many ways. I have used spreadsheets and software specific to my industry. Whatever you decide to use, just make sure that you stick with it. Block out time weekly to update your tracking. Doing so more frequently will be much easier than once a year!

Tracking your business activity will give you information you can use to make minor adjustments in the future to significantly impact your bottom line. Doing this will help you truly run your business like a business.

Key chapter takeaways:

- Determine what business metrics are important to you, and track them
- Block out time weekly to track your business
- Block out time weekly to review your plan
- Block out time at different points throughout the year to review and make adjustments to your goals and plan

Resources:

- Microsoft Excel or industry-specific business tracking software

CHAPTER THREE:

BUDGETING AND TAXES

How much should you invest in your business? How much do you need to set aside for taxes? Should you take a salary or an owner's distribution? How much should you keep in your business's reserve account? Sometimes it feels like so many questions need to be answered when it comes to the "financial" part of your business. In this chapter we will address some of those questions. We will review the importance of creating and operating under a budget and some important tips for saving and planning for your taxes.

Ever since that stint in my first sales role, I have been contributing some percentage of my hard-earned revenue toward my business. In the beginning, it wasn't much (maybe 1–2% of revenue), and I didn't have a clear plan for how to use it to grow my business. If I wanted to do it, I would just pay for it, rather than budgeting for activities aimed at growth. That was ok when the expenses were a couple thousand dollars a year and it was a very small percentage of my revenue. (Well, it really wasn't "ok.") But now, as the expenses and investment into the business have increased dramatically, I have to budget and plan.

It's hard to know how much money to invest in your new or even "mature" business. *Note*: "Mature" is a relative term, and it could mean something different for each person reading this. I define it as when the business owner is no longer actively trying to grow their business. Rather they just maintain it.

I have heard various rules for how much to reinvest into your business. Once, someone recommended that I **reinvest 30% of my earnings back into my business** because I am still trying to grow it. I believe you just have to be realistic. If you are in a growth phase of your business, you will need to invest more than if you are in a maintenance or "mature" phase.

You might wonder what activities I have done or implemented to grow my business. We will discuss that in Chapter Six: Marketing!

Some months, you might put 35% of the revenue back into the business, while other months, you may put 15% back in. The important point to remember is to **have a target** of what percentage you will reinvest each and every month.

If you are an individual business owner and not in a partnership situation, balancing reinvesting in the business and the expenses you might have in your personal life can be a challenge. When you are an individual business owner (typically what's called a "sole proprietorship"), a very blurry line separates the personal from the business. As there is no clear cut separation between the business and your personal life, budgeting is even more important.

In your business—just like in your personal life—you will have fixed expenses and variable expenses. When creating your budget, start by listing your fixed expenses. You might have expenses like:

- Software subscription fees
- Rent or lease payments
- Utilities

Once you've listed the fixed expenses you anticipate having, list the variable expenses. They could be items like:

- Postage
- Advertising/Marketing
- Payroll (if you have employees; if not, this would also be for yourself)
- Taxes

Once you have the initial list of anticipated business expenses, you can write in dollar amounts for each category. If you are just starting out, you may have to use your best guess and refine the numbers as you have more supporting data a month or two later. ***Make these adjustments to your budget during the time you have blocked out periodically to review your plan.***

We should pause for a minute and talk about how to track the finances for your business. If you are working with an accountant already, ask them if they have a preferred software for you to use. If they do, this can help with the tax return preparation for the business because it makes the information easy to provide the accountant and in a format they are already comfortable with.

If you don't have an accountant or they don't have a recommended software program, a number of options are available. You can always use an Excel spreadsheet which, in the beginning, would be cost-effective and pretty easy (depending on your comfort level with Excel). Or, start out using a product like Quicken or QuickBooks. If you get in the habit of using programs like these from the very beginning, you won't have to spend a lot of time transferring data to these as your business grows and it becomes necessary to use a software program for your finances.

I use Quicken for my personal finances and QuickBooks for my business finances. Both are great tools and work well for what I am trying to accomplish. Remember though, they are only a tool. They will provide you with as little or as much data related to the finances of your business as you want, depending on how much data you ultimately enter. Spend a little time researching the different software options, available and find one that you are comfortable with that you believe will fit your needs.

Once you decide how to track the finances for your business, enter the categories you came up with and the dollar amounts assigned to each category into the software. This is the beginning of your budget!

I alluded to adding a tax component to your variable expense category list. It's important that you do have this category included as you will have to allocate and save a portion of your revenue to cover this area. As a business owner, for any revenue you generate, not only are you responsible for the employee's share of taxes but also the employer's share. Under current tax law, budget and save *an additional 7.65%* of your revenue to cover the employer's share of federal FICA taxes for Social Security and Medicare.

Do some research online or check with your accountant to get a complete list of the taxes you may need to pay. Each state will be a little different, depending on the state and, if applicable, local tax rates. *I estimated that I needed to set aside about 40% of any gross revenue I generated for taxes, and then what was left over could be allocated to my business and personal expenses.* It sure doesn't feel like much is left after the taxes have been withheld, but unfortunately, that's the way it is.

Typically, tax payments as a business owner are made quarterly. Therefore, you have to save the money you withheld for taxes until it's time to submit the funds. I *highly* recommend creating a separate checking or savings account specifically for your tax deposits. For me, this helped me create a different mindset around these funds. By having the additional account just for tax withholding, you know the only expense the money in the account can be used for is taxes. It's very easy to fall into the trap of "robbing Peter to pay Paul" and if you "borrow" from the tax account, you could run the risk of not paying the account back and also not having enough for your quarterly tax submission. Don't mess with the IRS!

I must confess, I have "borrowed" money from my tax account and struggled to pay it back. What this tells me is that *I didn't have a properly funded reserve account*. When you are a business owner, your income can fluctuate. You might have some amazing months of income and some really dismal months of income. A properly funded reserve account can help level out your income and keep the bills paid during the slow months.

I recommend having at least six months' worth of expenses saved in this account. Knowing what your monthly budget looks like helps you determine what this number should be. So, when you generate revenue in excess of your expenses during one month—including the base salary you determined you needed to take—put the excess revenue into this account until you hit that goal.

Just make sure that you pay attention to the balance in this account. If you need to access it, then remember to replenish it when the next good revenue month occurs.

Let's talk about your salary and how you should "take" it. The structure of your business entity will, to some extent, dictate how you should take your salary. Talk with your accountant or CPA to determine the best structure for your business entity.

If you provide consulting services, you might receive income from other companies as an independent contractor or be a 1099ed professional. Under current tax law, if you receive less than $600 from that business, you may not receive a 1099, but it doesn't mean you don't have to report it on your tax return!

When I started out, the IRS website was very helpful for me to understand the tax rules and what I should and shouldn't be doing as a business owner. I recommend spending some time on their site at www.irs.gov.

If you are working with an accountant or CPA, make sure to set up a meeting with them to talk about how best to "hit the ground running." As an example, keep proper documentation of expenses related to your business because you may reap some tax benefits from it. You'd be surprised by what expenses you can deduct for your business! By maintaining the proper documentation, you also have proof that those expenses were truly business related, in case the IRS ever audits your records.

KEEP YOUR RECEIPTS!

Budgeting and planning your finances will help reduce financial stress both in your business and personal life. It will help create more consistent cash flow and will generally give you a better understanding of what it will take to run your business consistently from a financial standpoint.

Key chapter takeaways:

- Create your budget
- Use software to manage your finances
- Create and fund an operating reserve account with six months of expenses in it (including your salary)
- Do not commingle tax payments with operating funds—use a separate account for your tax payments
- Use an accountant or CPA that you believe will benefit you and the business

Resources:

- www.irs.gov
- Your accountant or CPA
- Software that can help track, organize, and manage your business finances

CHAPTER FOUR:

SYSTEMS/PROCESSES/PRACTICE MANAGEMENT

I have a dream... This dream is what my business will look like in the future. This dream is vivid with smells, colors, and sounds. I can see myself walking through this office, and I hear the bustling of people in the office, the sounds of the phone ringing and copy machine running. I see the positioning of desks and seating area for clients.

As I think about what needs to happen for me to get closer to realizing this dream, I have also come to understand that it's about the *experience* that's created. The interactions we have with associates, employees, clients, and potential clients create an experience for them. That experience can either be a positive or negative one. In this chapter we will talk about creating the client/customer experience you envision through the systems and processes you put in place.

What type of experience do you want to create? Can you "see" it? Can you hear and smell it? **Whatever experience you create for your clients or associates is unique to you and your vision.**

However, the experience shouldn't be unique to each person you interact with: the experience should be *consistent and repeatable* every single time. Why? When you start out as a new business owner, having systems in place that enable you to repeat the process can help you gain confidence. I have noticed for myself that the more I "know" the material, the more comfortable I am and the more confidently I can deliver the message.

But, what happens when you ultimately expand and you hire someone? You have to start from ground zero in teaching and explaining all the steps that you have implemented to date to that new person. What if you had processes that were clearly defined and written?

Think about McDonalds as an example. (One of my secret guilty pleasures by the way . . . I know, I know, so unhealthy.) If you have ever eaten there, regardless of location, you know what to expect. You can always expect the same hamburger with the same three pickles and the same amount of mustard and ketchup. How do you think this happens? Employees follow a step-by-step guide on how to build that hamburger. What's amazing when you think about McDonalds (regardless of how you feel about the food) is that they have a step-by-step set of instructions for everything that happens there. THIS is what helps create the consistency and efficiency we all hope to develop in our businesses.

To create a consistent experience, you HAVE to create written processes for what you consider to be the critical components of your business.

Start by listing those components. Here are a few examples of processes that are important in my business:

- Client onboarding
- Client service standards
- Annual client review meetings
- Weekly staff meeting agenda
- Script for answering the phone

The above are specific for me. Depending on your business, these could look very different. Regardless, take some time, and start writing down the processes you want to make sure are consistent and repeatable.

Once you have written out the initial list of processes or systems, next write out the step-by-step instructions for completing that process. Write the instructions as if you were explaining it to someone with no experience or knowledge of your industry. Don't use industry jargon or skip over steps because you might think it's self-explanatory. This will be helpful in the future if you hire an employee because, remember, we all started at some point with little to no experience.

Once you have written out what you believe is a complete, step-by-step process, ask an "outsider" to review the written procedure. I would define the "outsider" as a person with no experience in your business or industry.

We joke in my office that we have an "SOP" (or "standard operating procedure") for EVERYTHING! I had to laugh as I was thinking about that because we even have an SOP for how to use the postage machine . . . Ok, first of all, I can never remember the code for the postage machine, so it saves me time by not needing to look it up. Second, I don't want to have to train a new person on how to use the postage machine, and third, I have other, more important things to do than figure out how to use the postage machine each time I want to send something!

All joking aside, creating these operating procedures early on will help with efficiency and actually save you time later. (And I really do have an SOP for the postage machine! ☺)

As your business grows or as you evolve, you may want to adjust your systems and processes. Once a calendar year, take some time to review and make changes to your procedures. Or, if you are practicing a 90-day "year" review one fourth of your written procedures every three months.

Remember, this is YOUR business, and it is a reflection of you.

I have found a great resource for all of this is the book: *The E-Myth Revisited: Why Most Small Businesses Don't Work and What to Do About It* by Michael E. Gerber. I absolutely LOVE this book, and it has had a huge impact in helping me create a consistent, meaningful experience for those I interact with.

Let's switch gears a little bit and talk about practice management and maintaining client information. Wouldn't it be great if you had a software program that maintained all of your client's contact information and gave you the ability to input notes or other important information related to your client? When I first started out, I didn't think too much about this. I was mostly concerned about paying my bills and making sure the business actually survived. I was missing part of the big picture, though, in not capturing information early on.

Having a "central" location to store client's contact information, purchase information, likes, dislikes, and other demographics saves you time, ultimately, and gives you other opportunities for marketing in the future.

Think about this. I am in a service industry. When I meet a person, the person ultimately "buys" one of two things: 1. The service I'm offering, and 2. Me. So I have to set my business apart from all the others that offer a similar service.

At the receptionist's desk, I keep a list of the clients I will see that day and—if they have been in before—what drink they requested previously. When a client walks into my office, the receptionist greets them by name and asks if they would like such and such to drink again. Right away, we create a unique experience for the client because we remember! Like I said before, though, I have a husband, three kids, three cats, employees, and a business to run. If I met with the client two months ago, I certainly wouldn't remember what they ordered to drink, but my software will!

Find a software program that you find easy to use and can capture the customer or client information you believe is important. Doing this will give you the ability to market to your clients in the future, increase the personal "touches" to clients and help create that unique experience. Start early with this, and it will provide you with much fruit in the future!

Start with a client relationship management software program early on instead of using paper or Outlook or Excel. It might cost some additional money, but it's a heck of a lot easier using the software from the beginning instead of going back later and building it when you have hundreds of clients.

I've mentioned a couple times that I have three cats. What I didn't mention, though, is that I LOVE cats. Total crazy cat lady here! Doesn't it always seem to be the case that when you are really passionate about something you tend to find others who are also equally as passionate?

I bring this up because my love of cats is a great example of how you could use that information in the future. I made a note in my client database software of all my crazy cat lady clients, and now I have created a niche I can market to. My software makes it easy to generate a report of all the people I've entered into that category. No more trying to remember or manually put together a mailing list. If you code your client database, it makes it really easy to market to everyone later.

I still haven't figured out what to do for all of my crazy cat lady clients, but you better believe I'm working on something big!

Key chapter takeaways:

- Create standard operating procedures for those processes you want to replicate
- Have an "outsider" review your written processes
- Find and use a software program to maintain and capture client information
- Determine what information you will gather on each client

Resources:

- *The E-Myth Revisited: Why Most Small Businesses Don't Work and What to Do About It* by Michael E. Gerber

CHAPTER FIVE:

HIRING AND MANAGING STAFF

So you've been growing your business and spending more and more hours at or on work with no end in sight. The to-do list just keeps getting longer and longer, and you feel like you are being pulled away from the most important aspects of the business. Is it time to hire someone? Is it time to add someone to the team? Can you afford it? Can you afford not to? These can be very difficult and scary questions to answer, so I'm devoting this chapter to just that.

I remember hiring my first staff person. *I was petrified*. There were so many thoughts running through my mind and definitely a lot of second guessing. Could I afford it? Could I keep them busy? Did I have all the right things in place? (I didn't really even know what those "things" were.) Do I have enough time to manage, sell, train, and keep the business running? How would I know if the decision was successful and worthwhile?

What ultimately motivated me enough to hire someone was that *I was just plain tired*. I was tired from working all the extra hours on the administrative parts of the business, knowing that I also needed to continue to grow the business. I was tired from being the "jack of all trades" in my business. I was tired of losing time with my family instead of gaining time. When I finally hired that first person, I did so ultimately believing in myself. I had nothing else to go on.

Someone told me when I was first considering hiring someone that if I was using the time this person freed up to help grow the business and wasn't wasting the time, then it was a success. I shouldn't just hire someone so I could take more time off or screw around more. This statement made a lot of sense to me. Based on that, here are a couple questions you can ask yourself that will help you know if it's time to hire another person:

- Are you bogged down in administrative duties or functions that are keeping you from the primary aspects of growing your business?
- Do you know your hourly rate? This is the rate you would pay a person if you were hiring them to perform the core components of your business. Is this hourly rate more than what you would pay a person to do administrative or clerical work for you?

If you honestly answered "yes" to the above questions, then it's time to consider hiring someone.

Once you decide to hire another person, implement a few key components before that new person joins the team.

First, think about and commit in writing this person's job description. Even if you are hiring a summer intern, make sure you have a job description for this person. Having a written job description for any position you want to fill will help in communicating expectations, training, and performance reviews.

When I wrote the job description for that first administrative position, I spent a lot of time thinking about what I really wanted this person to do. I knew I wouldn't be able to cover everything in that first pass as it was an evolving role, but I did cover what I believed were the core functions.

To help in writing your job description, think about this: what do you hate to do in your business? In determining your hourly rate, what duties would you pay someone else a lower hourly rate for? In what areas of your business do you feel you might be weak; could having another person on board compliment and strengthen your areas of weakness?

Something else that you should think about and have in place prior to hiring someone is what benefits, if any, you want to offer. Having some sort of benefit package will help you be more competitive in the employment market and can also help with employee satisfaction and retention. Here are some common benefits that might be offered:

- Health insurance
- Short- or long-term disability income insurance
- Retirement plan
- Sick time
- Vacation time

You don't have to offer every benefit right away. Start small and continue to add. There is nothing wrong with that!

Prior to becoming an employer, you should also know your state's employment rules. What special requirements do you need to adhere to? When I first considered hiring someone, I literally just Googled "employment laws" for my state.

Lastly, how is your payroll going to be structured? Are you going to do this in-house manually, use a bookkeeping or payroll service, or use payroll software? I work with a number of accountants and CPAs that offer payroll services. Utilizing their services can help save you a lot of time (and headache) from writing the paychecks, submitting the quarterly payroll filings, and taking care of all the other components that come with the territory. However, it can be costly, so make sure you know the cost ahead of time and work it into your budget.

I ultimately elected to use a payroll company that takes care of all the reporting and filing and has an online time clock for my employees to be able to clock in and out. It does require some administration on my part as I have to input the new employee's data into the software but it is relatively inexpensive and does not require a lot of time.

Once you have thought through these components and have them in place, you are ready to hire your first employee!

When I interviewed people in the past for an available position, I reviewed a lot of resumes. Some were impressive, and some were so-so. Just remember, "You can't judge a book by its cover." It doesn't hurt to talk to a number of potential applicants. Don't lose patience! I have found that because of my desire to solve the problem quickly, I have sometimes been too quick to hire. If you find yourself in a similar situation, I have a couple suggestions.

Hire slow; fire quick.

Hire for attitude; fire for skill.

These two statements have really helped me. I have discovered that, because of my desire to get back to work and expedite the hiring process, I have sometimes hired new employees too quickly. I have also been so impressed by a person's resume that I didn't take the time to conduct my due diligence in the interview process. Don't short change the process, and trust your instinct. Don't let instant gratification win out.

Remember, skill can be taught; attitude can't. How many times have you heard "everything I need to know I learned in high school or college"? Never? Yeah, me either.

I have often struggled with what questions to ask in the interview. Honestly, it depends on what you're looking for, so tailor your questions to the position you are trying to fill.

First, determine the personality profile you are looking for in the available position. If you need a detail-oriented person, ask questions that will help you determine if the candidate is detail-oriented. If you want to hire for a creative position, you will need to structure your questions to help best determine their creativity.

Here are a few questions that I typically ask during an interview:

1. Where do you see yourself in five years?
    a. I ask this in almost every interview because I want to hire someone that wants to be here five years from now. If I ask that question, and they say something completely different then, chances are, I am not going to hire them.

2. What did you like or dislike about your prior job?
    a. This goes a long way toward telling me about the candidate's attitude. Pay attention to the words they use to describe their last job. Are the words positive or negative?
3. What is your greatest strength? Your greatest weakness?
    a. This helps give you an idea of the areas they feel they are accomplished in and the areas they feel they need to improve. Does this compliment you and/or your company and the position available?
4. How would you describe yourself?
    a. This will help you decide how creative or detail-oriented they are.

I recently read an article that suggested asking the "where you see yourself" question is "old school" or not relevant any longer. Like I said before, create a list of questions that *you* believe will best help you determine the most appropriate candidate for the position you are trying to fill. Use your list of questions a number of times as you hire new employees, and adjust them if needed.

Many people have asked me how many times you should interview someone. I typically conduct a phone interview first and then have an in-person interview. I like having the phone interview in addition to the in-person because a lot of my work is done over the phone. I want to make sure this person will also be able represent me to the degree I'd like and can help create my vision regardless of the communication method.

Something else you have to consider prior to hiring someone is your policy on working with friends and family. Will you hire a friend? Will you hire a family member? Often when you go down this path, the boundaries between work and personal relationships can get crossed. What does this mean for your relationship with that person? What could this mean if you have other employees who *aren't* friends or family? Tread lightly if you decide to go down this path. Make sure you have very clear boundaries in place and that they are respected at all times.

I have a confession: I work with my husband. It can be a HUGE challenge because when I am upset about something that happened during our personal relationship, I know I shouldn't bring it into the workplace, and I'm not always successful with leaving it at home. I KNOW it has caused some discomfort for the other employees. Therefore, I have to work extra at keeping that separation between our personal and professional relationships. I will say, though, it can also be extremely rewarding because we often have lots to talk about, we both enjoy discussing different projects we are working on, and I definitely believe "two heads are better than one."

Once you have found and hired the right person for the position you want to fill, you can start training! Remember those standard operating procedures you wrote? These will come in handy in helping communicate expectations and training this new person.

Whenever you bring a new person on board, remember that you are now a team. You have to communicate! One of the biggest risks that people face when they have employees is lack of communication. You need to make sure you regularly provide feedback and communicate clear expectations.

Consider having a weekly team meeting or a 15-minute daily "huddle" to discuss important issues or items that need addressed or taken care of. Also consider having a regular performance review with your employee. This could be once a quarter, every six months, or once a year. This gives you both the opportunity to review the job description for that position and address areas of potential improvement and areas that are going really well.

I like to have employees participate in their performance reviews, so I ask them to answer the following questions and expect them to discuss them during the review meeting.

1. What were your biggest accomplishments since our last review?
2. What was your biggest challenge?
3. How did you do in relation to your goals for the last period?
4. What are your goals for the upcoming period?
5. What are some areas of improvement that you see for us/and or your position?

You will eventually have to evaluate their performance in the position, so having the written job description that you used to hire for the position can help you with the evaluation. You need to be prepared to discuss opportunities for improvement, as well as acknowledge areas they have excelled in. Always make sure you document the review and keep a record of it in their personnel file. Documenting the review will create the record to build from for the next review (so you don't have to remember what was discussed!).

I was once told to praise in public and reprimand in private. This was great advice, and it helps with employee satisfaction. During our extended weekly team meetings, I try to pick out something so I can acknowledge the employees in front of everyone else. I use the performance reviews to discuss areas of improvement.

Don't forget…if you have administrative staff, ***Administrative Professional's day is always the fourth Wednesday in April each year!***

It's nice to take time to formally acknowledge your employees for their contribution to making the business what it is today. I think of my employees like an extension of my family, so it's important to have fun together too! We take the time to have a monthly team lunch. Each month a different team member gets to pick where we eat. I pick up the tab, but it gives us all an opportunity to get to know each other a little more and, often, try new food.

The lunches are fun, but I think we all look forward to the team "bonding" day even more. Every quarter, we pick a different activity to do together. We block out the time on a Friday—the staff gets paid for the day—and we enjoy trying something different. This quarter, for example, we are going to shoot skeet. Talk about something completely different!

Speaking of something different and fun, do you know what I did last weekend? I spent several hours creating an employee handbook. That's how you know you've officially become a small business owner. Instead of going out with friends for a night on the town (not that I would have done that anyway, I have three kids, but you get the point) I stayed at home making sure my expectations and the policies that pertain to my employees were clear, concise, and in writing.

If you have one employee or fifty employees, develop an employee handbook. I started my handbook by Googling "employee handbook template." I didn't know how else to start. If anything, it gave me some good ideas on what should and shouldn't be included in the book. It also gave me good ideas of policies I wanted to have in place for my employees.

Once I had a good draft, I asked a local attorney who specializes in employment law to review the book for me. In my state, I am held to additional state-level employment rules because I exceed a certain number of employees. So, my employee handbook must be properly structured and signed off on by each employee.

Though we may not like the topic, on occasion, we don't hire the right person for a position, so ultimately we have to terminate the employee. The first time I terminated someone, I cried. It felt awful. I felt like I failed. I felt like the worst person in the world. If you do end up needing to terminate an employee, make sure you have good documentation. Your state may have specific rules about termination, as well, so make sure you check your state's employment rules.

All in all, that first step in deciding it's time to add someone to the team can be nerve-wracking. But, it can also be liberating and exciting. You may not know the exact best time to add an employee, but trust in yourself, and you won't go wrong.

Key chapter takeaways:

- Know your hourly rate
- Create and use job descriptions
- Consider the benefits you will offer
- Determine how payroll will be managed
- Don't short-change the interview process
- Create a system for effective communication
- Conduct regular reviews with employees
- Have and use an employee handbook

Resources:

- An employment law attorney
- Payroll software
- Your accountant or CPA

CHAPTER SIX:

MARKETING

What does it mean to grow your business? What are some ways a person can grow their business? Should you advertise or use word of mouth? What about direct mail or networking groups? Every day, we are marketing in some way, whether you think so or not. Marketing is always evolving as well, so it's important to pay attention to this area. In this chapter, we will talk about some of the different ways you can market your business and considerations when creating your marketing plan.

The first step in creating and having a successful marketing plan is determining what message you want to communicate to the public. Use your mission and vision statements to help you here. When I thought about this for myself, I realized that I really just want to help people. People can feel overwhelmed, frustrated, and frankly, afraid if their financial house isn't "in order," so it's my goal to help alleviate those feelings so they can focus on other areas of their lives. This is the bottom line for me. So, how do I best communicate that to the public?

Once you've determined the message, now you have to weave that into your brand and your communications to the public. *Remember, consistency is key!*

Do you have a logo and tagline? Do you think it represents you well? If you don't have your logo and/or tagline, consider working with a graphic designer or marketing consultant for this component.

I never realized that the colors you select for your logo represent different things. For example, did you know certain colors are used more frequently for restaurants than any other color? There are also certain font styles or scripts that can evoke different feelings when used. I have never considered myself to be very creative, so I did end up working with a graphic designer/marketing consultant for this. It was worth every penny! She spent a lot of time trying to understand what's important to me and the message that I wanted to convey to my potential clients. The logo that was ultimately created speaks to my heart. It was, in part, an homage to Montana and represents the mountainous journey we often trek as business owners, planning or saving for the future and so much more.

Whatever you create or created for your logo and/or tag line for your business, make sure you use them in *all* communications to the public.

Create a list of items that you will use regularly that require your logo. Here are some possible pieces:
- Letterhead
- Envelopes
- Business cards

Did you think of other pieces? After you create your list, divide the list between "essential" and "like to have." Have the essential pieces created first, and then as time and money allow, work on the others.

Marketing is always evolving, and today, technology is a huge component. I did not grow up using technology like people do today, so I have had a big learning curve with all the different social media sites out there. Social media is a *must* as part of any good marketing plan. The many different options can be a bit overwhelming, but here are the big ones to consider using:

- LinkedIn
- Facebook
- Twitter
- Pinterest (technically a search engine)
- YouTube

Recently, I held an event for which I mailed out hardcopy invitations. Someone told me that they didn't remember when the event was because they didn't get an event notification from Facebook. I hadn't set up the event on Facebook, and I won't make that mistake again!

Even though I didn't grow up using social media, I have forced myself to learn it and become more comfortable with it. If you are not using social media as part of your marketing plan, you are missing out on a lot of opportunity. I have gained somewhat of a comfort level with it and understand the importance of it, and I have NO desire to do much with it. So, I outsourced my social media component. I have a twenty-something-year-old who takes care of my digital media marketing on a part-time basis. They are much quicker with it than I am, and it eliminates stress from my life!

I've learned that just having the social media sites isn't enough either. You actually have to use them! So, I have started actively posting to my business Facebook page, my

LinkedIn page, and Twitter (well sometimes I do, but mostly it's my social media expert who does). We sit down once a week and schedule all the posts I want to do for the entire week. Many different applications are available to automatically post what you want for you at a scheduled time, which means you don't need to remember to post every day. I just schedule my post in the app, and it will automatically post the piece to whichever social media sites I have selected on the preset day and time.

I almost forgot . . . don't forget to use video messages, too! I have not ventured down this path yet, but it is in the plans. Posting short, educational videos (remember, most people's attention spans aren't that long) to your website and social media sites helps you gain credibility and also improves the search engine optimization. I recommend using a combination of pre-recorded videos and live videos. If you post live videos, make sure the audience can see you easily, so check your lighting first. Also, don't chew gum or fidget too much. It can be distracting and takes away from the message you are trying to convey.

Having a social media presence has become so important anymore that you may lose business if you do not have it. I spoke with someone recently who said they will look a company up through a search engine before they do business with them. If that company doesn't have a website, at a minimum, she wouldn't do business with that company. The lesson I took from that comment was that you MUST have a website. Don't expect it to actually "drum up" loads of business for you; however, it does act like a virtual business card and helps create credibility.

Not only do you need a website, but you also have to periodically post to your website, too. This helps with the search engine optimization (SEO) so when someone searches for your company, it will show up higher in the search results list.

In this age of technology and digital media marketing, some of us "old school" people still prefer to get mail. I have heard that mail campaigns have about a 1% response rate. I have tried a number of direct mail campaigns, and that pretty much held true for me too. Direct mail can be rewarding, but don't expect to send out just one piece and think you will get a bunch of responses. I recommend that you do any direct mail campaign over a 12-month period and actually send out one piece a month. Remember, it's about consistency!

Newsletters are also a great digital or direct mail marketing piece. They can be used to help educate consumers or potential customers on your product and your company. I have chosen to send out a quarterly newsletter because I send out other educational articles related to my field during the other months.

I spoke with another woman business owner who said she was more likely to read a newsletter if it was available digitally (so e-mailed to her or available through a social media site). I feel the opposite way. I am so bombarded with e-mails and other social posts that I don't end up reading many of them. I'm just the typical look-at-cute-cat-videos person. I will, however, read a piece of mail that comes to my home because, anymore, I just get bills and junk mail. So this tells me it is very important to understand your target market. You have to have a good handle on where they "hang out" and how they prefer to be marketed to.

Speaking of "old school", it used to be that just having a brick and mortar location with a good sign was all the marketing you needed to do. Does that still work now? I would contend that it's just not enough. Having a physical location for your business can help increase credibility; however, additional costs come with that. If your business is retail-oriented and you offer some tangible product, then having a physical location is necessary. But, if you are a service-oriented business, depending on the nature of the service, you could potentially run your entire business through Facebook. When it comes to a physical store front, it's still all about location, location, location to draw in your target market.

What about networking events? These can be a great way to also get the word out. In most cases, these seem to be about consistency, too. Don't expect to go to one networking event and come back with three new clients. You have to develop relationships with people, and that typically isn't done instantaneously. If you participate in a networking group and regularly attend, you will most likely find the opportunities are abundant. I recommend regularly attending one or two networking events that happen on a monthly basis. I would treat your in-person networking groups no different from any social media groups you might belong to. Just because you are a member, don't expect people to seek you out. You have to participate!

I learned recently about some additional capabilities available through Google. Did you know you can set up Google Alerts with different key words, and Google will search the internet based on the criteria you entered? By doing this, it gives me the ability to get alerts related to any target demographics I might have. How handy would that be when in conversation with someone that falls into that group, say that I might meet at a networking event?

If you elect to advertise, you will want to get the most "bang for your buck," so make sure the advertisements are seen by your target market. For example, if your target market is senior citizens, I wouldn't recommend only advertising on Facebook. If your target market is millennials, I wouldn't recommend only advertising in the newspaper.

I have dabbled in traditional advertising a bit, placing ads in television, radio, and print. TV ads were so expensive that I didn't do them for very long. As a small business owner, it just wasn't in my budget to continue with the program for the length of time it would take to really be beneficial. Advertising can help create a consistent message in different mediums, so it is definitely worthwhile. It is also my belief that, like direct mail, it takes time and, at least initially, has a low response rate.

In my industry, word of mouth and referrals have always been the best way to acquire new clients. I have found as well that if you don't ask, the client doesn't know you even *want* new clients. (Amazing, right?) Make sure that if you are going to ask for referrals that you have a *system* in place, and you work the system consistently. What does that mean? Know what you are going to say when asking for a referral. What are you comfortable saying?

I recently discovered that I am uncomfortable asking for a referral if that referral is for me, but I have NO problem asking for a referral if I am "helping" someone else out. So I have modified my referral ask language so I am still asking, but I'm tricking my brain into thinking I'm asking for someone else.

Any marketing plan has to be fluid and is always evolving. Make sure you keep track of the effectiveness of each of your marketing initiatives, like cost, new clients or sales generated, and time spent. As you get more data related to each of your marketing initiatives, you will find some that are more effective than others. As you learn which are the most effective, devote more time to those and reduce the time spent on others.

So much can be done under the guise of marketing that it can be overwhelming. Pick just two or three key marketing initiatives that you believe will be most impactful in your industry and to your target market. Keep in mind that a social media presence is a must, so implement some social media platforms 100% and evaluate their effectiveness after a period of time.

Remind yourself that the point of marketing is to convey your message to the public. How are you different from everyone else? How can you help? Just like with any part of your business plan, work the plan, and it will create much opportunity you can benefit from for years to come.

Key chapter takeaways:

- Create a logo and tag line that effectively convey your message
- Develop your necessary online presence with a website and social media sites

- Regularly post to your website and social media sites
- Consider either digital or physical newsletters
- Create credibility through advertising
- Attend one or two networking events consistently, both in-person and via social media
- Use consistent language when asking for referrals
- Track key data points related to each marketing initiative

Resources:

- Graphic designer and/or marketing consultant

CHAPTER SEVEN

PARTNERSHIPS/BUSINESS SUCCESSION

Have you ever thought about being in partnership with someone? How was your business idea created? Did you create it with a friend or family member? What is the reason you might want to partner with someone?

I too often entered into some of the partnerships in my past, both formal and informal, (and more than I'd like to admit) naïvely and woefully unprepared. I blindly partnered with someone, trusting everything would be ok and it would all work out. Had I asked more questions first, to make sure we were a good fit and that the foundation was good, it would have saved a lot of time, effort, and energy later. Let's spend some time in this chapter reviewing important considerations for partnering with another person.

Whenever you consider any type of partnership, always ask yourself a few questions first. Here are some of the most important:

1. What will you gain from having a partner?
   a. Will they complement you?
   b. Will they invest in the business?

   If you are not sure how they will complement you and the new business, DON'T DO IT.

2. What is your potential partner's work ethic? Could there be feelings of inequity given the number of hours you both would invest?

   Be careful with a partner who is not equally as committed to the venture as you are. You could have issues down the road after the initial excitement has worn off if one of you perceives that the work has not been equally distributed.

One of my past business partners and I were hosting a client event. It was at our office, so it required some set up prior to clients arriving. After working the entire day, the staff and I started setting up for the event, but my partner was nowhere to be found. We called their cell phone a couple times and finally got an answer. The now ex-business partner was at the bar having a couple cocktails before the event! Let me tell you—that was the beginning of the end.

3. What will each of your roles and responsibilities be?

   Just like when you hire a new staff person, you need to make sure that you and your potential partner are clear on division of duties and responsibilities.

4. Have they historically honored their commitments?

   It's important to make sure the potential partner shares the same values as you. Otherwise, this could create problems down the road.

5. What questions do they have?

Having a successful partnership requires open/honest communication. Your potential partner should feel that they have this with you.

6. Will they commit to everything in writing?

I would not enter into a partnership with someone who is not willing to make it legal. Having a written partnership agreement protects both of you.

7. What happens if it doesn't work out? What is the exit strategy?

It's important to have this conversation in the beginning before anything happens. Trying to unwind a partnership without an exit strategy in place can be challenging and tricky, especially when emotions get involved.

A partnership is like a marriage to some degree. When the honeymoon phase is over and the divorce is impending, a prenuptial agreement would have made things a lot easier for that couple getting divorced. A properly written exit strategy in your business partnership agreement will help you both transition more smoothly and quickly back to being "single."

When you are both ready to commit to the partnership in writing, here are some items that are often overlooked and should always be addressed in your written agreement.

- **Death**—what happens if one of you passes away prematurely?

- **Disability**—what happens if one of you becomes disabled and is no longer able to work in the business?
- **Divorce**—what happens if your partner is married and subsequently becomes divorced? If the soon to be ex-spouse is entitled to half of the marital assets, then they could be entitled to half of your partner's share of the business. That means you have brought on a new partner, unless this contingency is addressed in your agreement.
- **Disagreement**—as I referenced earlier in this chapter, make sure you have addressed and created the exit strategy for the partnership from the very beginning.
- **Valuation**—how will each partner's share of the company be valued?

An often missed detail in partnership arrangements is the valuation of the business. This is extremely important as it assigns a dollar value to your share of the partnership. If you or your partner decide to exit the partnership and the remaining partner wants to continue the business they would buy you out of your share. If you pass away prematurely, your partner would buy your estate out of your share. Including some sort of formula in your agreement that spells out how the business will be valued is critical. Over the years, I have heard of a number of different methods that could be used. The most important component, though, to valuing the business is consistency; especially when it comes to your partnership agreement. Whichever method you agree to include in your agreement should be what you use every time. I will not give any specific examples here of how to value your business as each industry will have its own unique formula.

I highly recommend working with an attorney to draft your partnership agreement and help you determine the most appropriate valuation method for your business.

Once your partnership has begun, here are some recommendations for maintaining a healthy partnership:

1. Have regular meetings to discuss the status of the business and any issues that arise.
2. Regularly discuss your roles and responsibilities and make adjustments as needed.
3. Discuss any staff issues together.

Communication is key!

A business partnership is like a marriage. You have to work on it regularly to maintain it and keep it healthy.

Key chapter takeaways:

- Have a written partnership agreement that includes an exit strategy
- Have a formula for valuing your business
- Conduct regular meetings with your partner to review the business

Resources:

- An attorney that specializes in partnerships and business succession plans

CHAPTER EIGHT

CHALLENGES, RECHARGING, AND REWARDING SUCCESS

think the universe is trying to tell me something...I am finding this to be THE MOST challenging chapter to write.

As women, we tend to take care of everyone else before ourselves. We often give until there isn't anything left to give. We don't typically take time to celebrate our successes because there is always something else that needs to be done. As I write this, it's currently 4:30 a.m., I'm exhausted, I still have to make lunches for my kids for school, get ready for work, and make sure everyone else is ready and out the door on time. **What about me?** In this chapter, we will talk about overcoming challenges, "recharging your batteries," and celebrating successes.

I recently started attending a women's business owners mastermind group. The intent is not for networking but rather creating a space to safely share and discuss issues or challenges one might be having in their business at the time. We also use it as a place to intentionally devote time to educating ourselves on practices that can help improve our business. Sometimes, while working in our businesses, we don't take the time to do some of these important things to help us grow.

This group has been instrumental in helping me feel a sense of belonging, security, and compassion, which I realize now that I had been missing. Often, being a woman business owner can feel very lonely. I didn't realize before coming to this group that, regardless of industry, women business owners often struggle silently through their stresses. This group changed that for me. I highly recommend joining a group like this, even if you have to create this space yourself with other like-minded women. What a great way to engage with other business-oriented women who most likely face similar challenges to your own.

A number of groups for business owners are available through different social media sites. I belong to groups through Facebook and LinkedIn. I like adding the different social media groups because it broadens the pool of collective knowledge and is not limited by geographic location.

I have also had mentors throughout the years or friends in my same industry who I can use as a sounding board. Having a mentor can help enhance your journey down the path of owning your business and creating your vision. A mentor is someone who has walked the talk, someone you aspire to be like. My mentor tells me like it is and has years of experience owning her own business. I can gain valuable insight from her experience. I typically meet with my mentor once a quarter and draft a list of items to discuss with her.

A mentor is someone different from an accountability partner (whom I also have!). An accountability partner is someone you have a quick daily or weekly conversation with to help you stay on track. Are you completing the tactics and goals that you committed to doing? If not, what's getting in the way? What can be done differently that will increase your chances of accomplishing those goals or tactics? I encourage you to have both a mentor and an accountability partner.

I have to admit that I am having a hard time feeling authentic in writing this chapter because recharging and celebrating success are things I struggle with so much. Once I've accomplished something, I don't stop because I have to make sure I take care of the next thing on the list. But, what I have learned is to just take baby steps. It's the little things that can help us stay motivated and focused and keep us from burning out.

I am an introvert at heart, so I recharge best when I have a quiet space with no interruptions. Of course, my cats coming to cuddle with me ALWAYS helps me relieve stress and re-center. I also love working in my garden, and let me tell you, I am able to vent A LOT of frustration on those weeds!

Here are some other ideas that have helped me refocus and bounce back:
- Read a few pages in an inspirational book
- Sit outside (a little vitamin D is good for all of us)
- Create a gratitude jar and put a note in each day or periodically for what you were thankful for on that day
- Take a walk (exercise is always helpful in relieving stress)
- Just sit back and take some deep breaths
- Meditate
- Write out your wins for the week (this will help you focus on the positive)

- Visualize what you see your business looking like next week or next year

So what are those little things that you hold precious?

It's the little things you do that will get you through until you have time to take vacation.

At the beginning of each 90-day period, I look at the quarter and determine if I will take any vacation days. Now as a business owner, you and I both know, you don't get paid vacation time, but it's still important to unplug, get away, and relax! I have just now (after 20 years) actually gotten to the point where, when I go on vacation, I will turn my phone off and not check e-mails or voicemails. I turn my out-of-office assistant on for my e-mail and change the voicemail on my phone to specifically say I DO NOT check while I'm out. You HAVE to take the time to unplug and not think much about work. It can be consuming if you don't give yourself that break.

Remember, as women we are often the coordinators for many different aspects of our lives both personally and professionally. If you don't take care of yourself, what good are we to all the other people who depend on us?

Some days, though, no matter how hard we might try, nothing seems to go right. Those days, I just want to stay in bed. When that happens, I don't set high expectations for myself; rather, it's my goal to JUST GET OUT OF BED. Just put one foot in front of the other and get through the day. That's OK! We can't always be Super Woman.

Sometimes, though, I have accomplished more than I expected or hit a goal that I thought was unattainable. When achieving things you thought were out of reach, reward yourself, too. It's important.

One easy way to reward yourself for a job well done is to schedule "break out time" during the work week. This is time you intentionally schedule yourself out of the office for a couple to a few hours. Maybe it's a Friday afternoon to get a massage or go hit golf balls. Whatever it is that you deem to be a treat, use it as a reward when you've hit your goals.

It's so important to have your network of support, to take time to reward yourself when you've done more than you thought you could, and not to give up. Take a minute to just give yourself the proverbial "pat on the back" because you deserve it!

Key chapter takeaways:

- Create your list of small things you can do to recharge
- Schedule your break out time
- Schedule your vacation
- Take time to unplug
- Join a group of like-minded individuals, either in-person or via social media to help you recharge, find comradery, and meet mentors or accountability partners

Resources:

- Accountability partner
- Mentor

- Professional group

CHAPTER NINE

CONCLUSION

Thank you for taking the time to read my tips for starting your journey in the world of business ownership and entrepreneurship. At times, I would have rather cleaned the *toilet* than write this because it made me relive the mistakes and past decisions I made. Talk about feeling vulnerable! But, in traveling with me for a bit through my journey in being a business owner, I hope you saw the love and support I feel for you. It was my goal to provide a place for you to feel *real*, to have doubts, to feel the fear, and to be able to keep going. I hope you find in this the motivation and support you need to continue on your path. You are not alone!

Use this book as a resource, write in it, tear pages out, and highlight the heck out of it! It's here to help you however you need it.

Connect with me on Facebook at Melanie Colusci - Author or www.fromstartuptosuccess.com so I can help continue to support you in your entrepreneurial journey.

KEY CHAPTER TAKEAWAYS AND RESOURCES

Chapter 1 – Having a Plan:
- Write a business plan
- Create your mission and vision statement
- Review your plan regularly
- Have clear, concise, measureable goals
- Time block!

Resources:
- *12 Week Year* by Brian Moran and Michael Lennington

- *The Secret* by Rhonda Byrne

- U.S. Small Business Administration www.sba.gov

Chapter 2 – Reviewing Your Plan/Tracking Progress:
- Determine what business metrics are important to you, and track them
- Block out time weekly to track your business
- Block out time weekly to review your plan
- Block out time during different points throughout the year to review and make adjustments to your goals and plan

Resources:
- Microsoft Excel or industry specific business tracking software

Chapter 3 – Budgeting and Taxes:
- Create your budget
- Use software to manage your finances
- Create and fund an operating reserve account with six months of expenses in it (including your salary)
- Do not commingle tax payments with operating funds – use a separate account for your tax payments
- Use an accountant or CPA that you believe will benefit you and the business

Resources:
- www.irs.gov
- Your accountant or CPA
- Software that can help track, organize, and manage the finances of your business

Chapter 4 – Systems/Processes/Practice Management:
- Create standard operating procedures for those processes you want to replicate
- Have an "outsider" review your written processes
- Find and use a software program to maintain and capture client information
- Determine client information you will gather on each client

Resources:
- *The E-Myth Revisited: Why Most Small Businesses Don't Work and What to Do About It* by Michael E. Gerber

Chapter 5 – Hiring and Managing Staff:
- Know your hourly rate
- Create and use job descriptions
- Consider the benefits you will offer

- Determine how payroll will be managed
- Don't short change the interview process
- Create a system for effective communication
- Conduct regular reviews with employees
- Have and use an employee handbook

Resources:
- An employment law attorney
- Payroll software
- Your accountant or CPA

Chapter 6 – Marketing:
- Create a logo and tag line that effectively convey your message
- A website and social media sites are a must
- Regularly post to your website and social media sites
- Consider either digital or physical newsletters
- Advertising can create credibility
- Attend one or two networking events consistently, both in-person and via social media
- Use consistent language when asking for referrals
- Track key data points related to each marketing initiative

Resources:
- Graphic designer and/or marketing consultant

Chapter 7 – Partnerships and Business Succession:
- Have a written partnership agreement that includes an exit strategy
- Have a formula for valuing your business
- Conduct regular meetings with your partner to review the business

Resources:

- An attorney that specializes in partnerships and business succession plans

Chapter 8 – Challenges, Recharging, and Celebrating Successes:
- Create your list of small things you can do to recharge
- Schedule your break out time
- Schedule your vacation
- Take time to unplug
- Join a group of like-minded individuals either in-person or via social media to help you recharge, find comradery, and meet mentors or accountability partners

Resources:
- Accountability partner
- Mentor
- Professional group

ABOUT THE AUTHOR:

Inspired by the women business owners she works with, Melanie has devoted her time to sharing her experiences with other inspiring female entrepreneurs. Melanie discovered that the driving factor for her success is derived from the development and execution of a long-term vision for her business, as well as a structured plan to get there. Melanie does the same for her clients. She connects them to what is possible and helps them create a plan to make possible a reality.

Melanie earned the CERTIFIED FINANCIAL PLANNER™ designation in 2003 and the Accredited Estate Planner™ designation in 2016. She is currently a member of the Executive Women's Council in Pittsburgh, the National Association of Women Business Owners, the Pittsburgh Women's Mastermind, and Women in Insurance and Financial Services. Melanie is also a multi-year award winner and has been featured in both the Wall Street Journal and, most recently, Forbes Wealth Managers Black Book magazine.

Originally from Bozeman, Mont., Melanie moved to Pittsburgh, Pa., in 2008.

While she is very passionate about her work, she savors every minute she has with her husband, three boys, and three cats. They spend their free time camping, swimming, and playing outdoors.

www.ingramcontent.com/pod-product-compliance
Lightning Source LLC
Chambersburg PA
CBHW020845210326
41598CB00019B/1972